# PUZZLE HUNTS
## for
## Reading Comprehension

## BY JILL GARRISON

Crystal Springs
SDE BOOKS
a division of Staff Development for Educators
Peterborough, New Hampshire

Published by Crystal Springs Books

A division of Staff Development for Educators (SDE)

10 Sharon Road, PO Box 500

Peterborough, NH 03458

1-800-321-0401

www.crystalsprings.com

www.sde.com

Published 2006

Printed in the United States of America

10 09      2 3 4 5

ISBN: 978-1-884548-86-4

Editor: Sharon Smith

Art Director, Designer, and Production Coordinator: Soosen Dunholter

Illustration at top of page 8 by Joyce Rainville. All other illustrations by Tina Rogers

**To Tina Rogers, a great friend,
without whom this book could
never have become a reality**

# CONTENTS

# ACKNOWLEDGMENTS

I would like to thank my son, my parents, my sister's family, and my many friends for their support and enthusiasm! Thank you to my editor, Sharon Smith, for taking my homespun ideas and turning them into a great book. I'd also like to acknowledge the hundreds of teachers, professors, school staff members, and administrators who have positively influenced my career in so many ways. Finally, thanks to all the students who helped me make this book a reality.

# HOW TO USE THIS BOOK

As a language arts and reading teacher for more than ten years, I have dealt firsthand with the frustrations of students still struggling with their reading in the middle grades—so I was as pleased as my students to discover how enthusiastically they responded to Puzzle Hunts. Students at all ability levels seem to like the idea of solving a puzzle; approaching reading as a "hunt," with a final goal in mind, makes the task a lot more fun. When they're engaged with the hunt, all students get a chance to practice important reading-comprehension skills, and struggling readers have an incentive to stay on task longer. (For ideas on differentiating instruction for different ability levels, see page 12.) As long as you set expectations appropriately, everyone has a chance to experience success.

## Classroom Materials Needed for Puzzle Hunts

- Photocopies of desired Puzzle Hunts for each student, with the drawing for each hunt on one page and the directions for it on a separate sheet(s)
- Colored pens/pencils/markers
- Graphite pencils for all non-colored markings
- Some of the puzzles also call for other reference tools, such as dictionaries, thesauri, or atlases.

## WHERE DO YOU BEGIN?

Before introducing the puzzles themselves, you may want to review with your students some of the skills they should be practicing before, during, and after reading. To help with that review, turn to page 13 and the master for "Reading Strategies to Use Every Day." Make one copy on a transparency; then make one paper copy for each student. With the master placed on the overhead and the students taking notes, have the class brainstorm strategies for each category, discussing what each strategy looks like and explaining when they might use it. Encourage students to discuss approaches they might use with any reading (textbooks, work sheets, the Internet, research assignments, etc.)—not just with the Puzzle Hunts.

As you and your students brainstorm reading strategies together, you might come up with a list that looks something like the illustration at right.

## THE ORDER MATTERS— SOMETIMES

Once the review is completed, students can move on to the fun part: the puzzles. The first Puzzle Hunt, "Tools for Success," is designed as a reminder of important elements in the reading process. It can also be a convenient introduction to the concept of Puzzle Hunts and how the ones in this book work. For those reasons, I've found it helpful to use this particular hunt first, and to follow up by giving each student a copy of the bookmark on page 17. The bookmark is a tangible reminder to continue to use these tools with all reading. Depending on the class, you may also find it beneficial to discuss and reteach these reading strategies before students begin each new Puzzle Hunt.

**Tools for Successful Reading**

**Level**
...out your learning with pictures, symbols and graphs

**Saw**
...through difficult reading slowly

**Hammer**
...through the easy-to-understand reading

**Chisel**
...into extra resources (dictionary, thesaurus, Internet)

**Clamp**
...onto information by rereading

**Drill**
...and review for tests

---

**READING STRATEGIES TO USE EVERY DAY**

Before Reading I Should:

*Read and/or listen to directions*

*Look at titles, pictures, and graphs*

*Notice boldfaced and italicized words*

*Read any questions I'll be answering later*

During Reading I Should:

*Stop frequently and paraphrase*

*Reread unclear passages*

*Fill in answers when I am able*

*Look up or ask about anything I don't understand*

*Take notes*

After Reading I Should:

*Finish answering assigned questions*

*Finish notes*

*Tell what I read about, or review it in my own mind*

*Prepare assigned projects or presentations*

*Review and study what I've learned*

---

## It's a Puzzle, Not a Contest

This is not a competition to see who can finish first; struggling readers do not need that added pressure. They *do* need you to show your pleasure at their time on task and their willingness to do a good job reading. Some readers simply can't work fast, but they *can* stay on task and show improvement. That's what these Puzzle Hunts are designed to encourage.

The last activity, in which students are given an opportunity to write their own Puzzle Hunts, is designed to be used only after students have successfully completed at least four Puzzle Hunts. The goal of this activity, "Write Your Own Cupcake Puzzle Hunt," is to integrate writing into the language-development process. Since this activity is different from all the others, you may want to use a slightly different approach when introducing it. Consider assigning pairs of students to create the puzzles and allowing several class periods for editing and rewriting.

You may also want to tell students ahead of time that you'll be making photocopies of the Puzzle Hunts they create and letting their peers try out those puzzles. Knowing that someone else will be looking at their puzzles gives students extra motivation to do a good job. However, many students' puzzles may not turn out the way they'd hoped. Be sure to set high expectations for being positive with each other, and encourage students to help edit their peers' work rather than quit if a Puzzle Hunt isn't perfect.

In short, deciding the sequence in which you want to present the hunts can turn into a puzzle of its own. Here's one approach to solving that sequencing puzzle:

1) Begin by having the class fill in the list of reading strategies together.

2) Introduce the hunts to your students through the "Tools for Success" Puzzle Hunt.

3) Present students with individual copies of the bookmark.

4) Choose other hunts for students to complete, in whatever order best meets your needs and those of your students, with just two exceptions: Use "Write Your Own Cupcake Puzzle Hunt" only after students have had some experience with the puzzles, and use "A Realistic Rain Forest" only after they've completed "Ridiculous Rain Forest."

## CLASSROOM MANAGEMENT TIPS

What else do you need to know about using Puzzle Hunts in your classroom? First, I would strongly encourage you to complete each Puzzle Hunt yourself before giving it to students. This allows you to compare your finished product with the answer key at the back of the book.

Once you've done that, give each student a copy of the selected Puzzle Hunt, along with any other materials he'll need. Explain that words in bold italic are ones students may need to look up. As students work on the puzzles independently, have them line up silently at your desk if they need to confirm a hunch, ask a question, or show you their completed Puzzle Hunts. This gives you a chance to assess how well individual students are able (or not able) to read and interpret the directions for each hunt. You can then point students to the directions they need to reread and responses they need to revise. You may want to remind them: No skipping to the end! Be sure to explain that in order to solve each Puzzle Hunt, they need to follow all the directions.

Sending students back to reread and to correct their own work is vital to the primary purpose of these activities: practicing reading skills. Tell your students you will give them a chance or two to fix any errors on their own. Be sure they understand that when you send them back to try again, you are not trying to be too tough on them; rather, you believe they can be great puzzle solvers if they read and reread carefully. Remind them that the activity is supposed to be a fun way to practice the reading process—not to get the answers from classmates or the teacher. Encourage students to feel a sense of accomplishment when they finally solve a puzzle correctly.

## A Note About Standards

The National Council of Teachers of English (NCTE) and the International Reading Association (IRA) have established 12 standards for English language arts. This book can help your students meet some of those criteria. The standards, or parts of those standards, addressed in this book are:

1.  Students apply a wide range of strategies to comprehend, interpret, evaluate, and appreciate texts. They draw on their prior experience, . . . their knowledge of word meaning . . . their word identification strategies, and their understanding of textual features.

2.  Students adjust their use of . . . written and visual language . . . to communicate effectively with a variety of audiences and for different purposes.

3.  Students apply knowledge of language structure, language conventions, . . . media techniques, figurative language, and genre to create . . .and discuss print and non-print texts.

4.  Students whose first language is not English make use of their first language to develop competency in the English language arts.

# ACCOMMODATIONS & ENHANCEMENTS

If you adapt your presentation of the material appropriately, Puzzle Hunts can be a great way to engage English language learners. Before giving these students the directions, try handing them just the drawings. Have ELL students identify the things in the drawings in both English and their native language. That will enhance their vocabulary readiness before they start on the puzzles.

When you work with ELL students, it's especially important for you to read and complete the lessons before you give them to your students. For these students, try highlighting terms or phrases that they may need help with before they read independently. Watch especially for figures of speech and culturally sensitive material (like an American holiday). Have students highlight those terms or phrases before they begin an activity, and make sure they understand what those words mean. A good picture dictionary can be helpful in this process.

Pairing, especially when you have a more fluent reader work with a less fluent one, can help to make a Puzzle Hunt a particularly effective learning tool for these students. Just be careful to monitor each pair to see that the less fluent student gets an opportunity to read and repeat the text and offer answers, even if she gives the answers in her primary language first.

You can also adapt the Puzzle-Hunt concept to make the hunts more challenging for particularly gifted students. Consider asking students which pictures are their favorites, then making extra copies of those. Assign students to write their own sets of directions for the drawings they've chosen. Another option is to ask each of your best (or most enthusiastic) artists to draw a scene and then have the class write about each of the student-generated drawings.

Whatever way you choose to differentiate in your classroom, I hope you'll find, as I have, that these puzzles truly do help to build strong, enthusiastic readers. I hope, too, that the students who complete these Puzzle Hunts in the future enjoy them as much as I've enjoyed creating them. If they also learn that reading can be fun, that sure can't hurt. Let the hunts begin!

# READING STRATEGIES TO USE EVERY DAY

**Before Reading I Should:**

_____

_____

_____

_____

**During Reading I Should:**

_____

_____

_____

_____

**After Reading I Should:**

_____

_____

_____

_____

# TOOLS FOR SUCCESS

Solve this Puzzle Hunt by helping Peg complete her bookshelves while you brush up on your reading skills.

Peg Board has helped out in her parents' woodworking shop just about all her life. Her dad, Chess Board, and her mom, Press Board, have asked her to make a bookshelf for all their manuals and trade books. Peg is excited to get to work on this project. She realizes that the process it takes to build something in the shop is a lot like the reading process her reading teacher is always talking about.

1.  BEFORE building her shelves, Peg must be sure that she has good instructions for what she wants to accomplish. She also must pull together all the materials she needs in order to complete the project. She knows she needs to do the same things before she starts reading.

2.  DURING the time Peg is working on her project, she sometimes has to stop and get more information. She goes back to her parents to find out what size shelves and what type of wood they want. This is a lot like what she does when she's reading. If Peg can read and understand things quickly, that's great, but sometimes she has to slow down, reread, and get more information (from a dictionary, for example) before she can fully understand what she's reading.

3.  AFTER Peg finishes building her shelves, she needs to sand them and then paint or stain them. If she didn't do that, the shelves would always seem unfinished. Peg decides this "finishing" step is a lot like what she does after reading: she checks over her work and goes back to the text for the answers to any questions she still has. If she didn't do that, her reading would be "unfinished"; she would have read the material but she wouldn't have made sense out of it.

Now it's time to match the following tools with their reading functions.

1.  Level : ___          A.  **dig into** extra resources like a dictionary,
                             thesaurus, or encyclopedia with this tool

2.  Saw: ___             B.  **spin things over and over** in your mind to review for
                             tests or to help you remember things

3.  Hammer: ___          C.  **keep things straight** by using pictures, symbols, and graphs

4.  Chisel: ___          D.  **slowly go through things that are difficult** to cut through

5.  Clamp: ___           E.  **nail down** the easy-to-understand material first

6.  Drill: ___           F.  **hold onto** new information and keep it in your mind
                             by rereading for better understanding

When you have finished this matching activity, go to the workbench picture and circle each of the six tools. Next, choose one or more words that best relate each circled tool to the reading function it represents. Write each of the word(s) on or next to the appropriate tool (for example, you may choose to write only the word "resources" on or next to a chisel).

Finally, show your teacher your finished work.

# I.

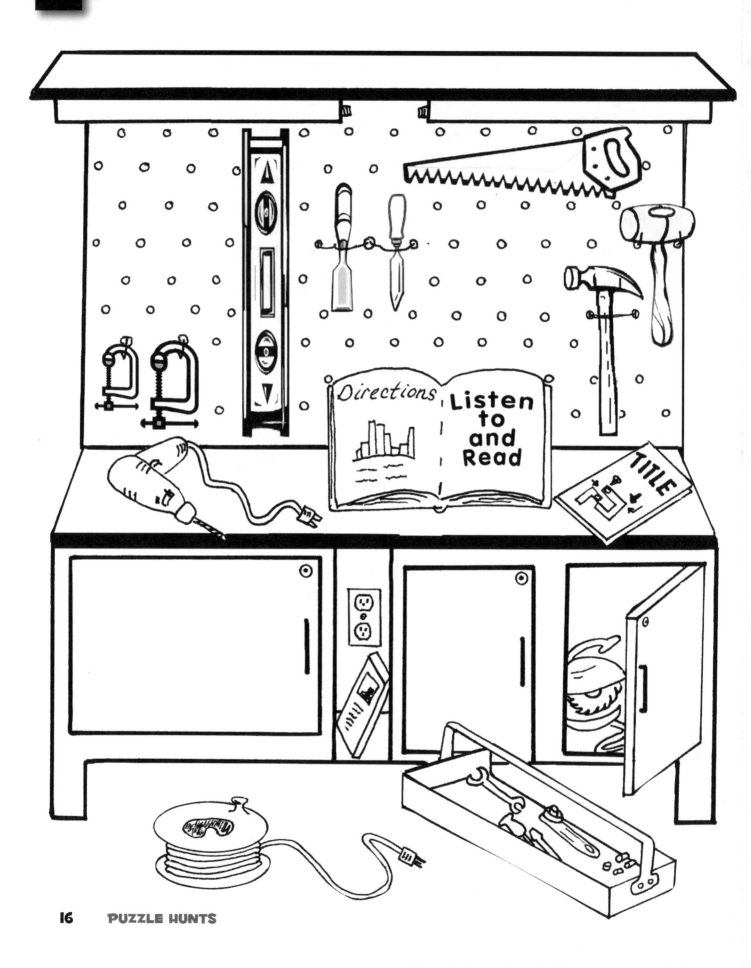

# READER'S BOOKMARK

Copy onto cardstock, cut out, laminate, and give to students to use as bookmarks.

## Tools for Successful Reading

**Level**
...out your learning with pictures, symbols and graphs

**Saw**
...through difficult reading slowly

**Hammer**
...through the easy-to-understand reading

**Chisel**
...into extra resources (dictionary, thesaurus, Internet)

**Clamp**
...onto information by rereading

**Drill**
...and review for tests

## Tools for Successful Reading

**Level**
...out your learning with pictures, symbols and graphs

**Saw**
...through difficult reading slowly

**Hammer**
...through the easy-to-understand reading

**Chisel**
...into extra resources (dictionary, thesaurus, Internet)

**Clamp**
...onto information by rereading

**Drill**
...and review for tests

# DINOSAUR IN DANGER

Use your great reading skills to figure out which dinosaur is in the most danger.

1.  There's a velociraptor in the foreground of this puzzle who seems pretty small, but he's about six feet long. His front claws are curved; some scientists believe he used those claws to hold onto his prey before finishing off the victim. Place a letter "V" on the velociraptor.

2.  A meat-eating dinosaur about forty feet long, the tyrannosaurus had teeth that measured up to six inches long. The *T. rex* in this hunt is standing near several palm trees. Write the word "carnivore" on this dinosaur.

3.  The pteranodon had no teeth; it is believed this dinosaur scooped fish up out of the water and swallowed them whole. Put a "Pt" above the pteranodon.

4.  What do the first three animals mentioned in this puzzle have in common? Were they **herbivores** or **carnivores**? Circle the correct word below and write that word's dictionary definition on the line.    herbivores    carnivores

   _____

5.  Although triceratops were ferocious-looking animals, scientists believe they were actually herbivores. Define **herbivore** on the line below. Then write "tri" below the animal with three horns on its head.

   _____

6.  The diplodocus was a long-necked dinosaur that ate leaves and then swallowed stones to assist in its digestive process. Write "herbivore" on the diplodocus that's behind the largest tree in the drawing.

7.  It is believed that this animal may have used its spiked tail for self-defense. The spikes on the body may have been for self-defense also, or they may have been a showy color to make this dinosaur attractive to potential mates. Write an "S" on this dinosaur, which is the stegosaurus.

8.  If you have followed the above directions, you should have just one animal left with no label. That animal, a twin to one you *have* already labeled, is in the gravest danger. Place an "X" on the dinosaur you haven't yet labeled and describe what danger you can infer it to be in.

   _____

# TEXT MESSAGE

It's 3:45 and school's over for the day. You just flipped your cell phone open to discover a text message waiting for you. To find out what's on your phone, read carefully through this Puzzle Hunt and follow the directions. As you work, fill in the blanks next to the cell-phone drawing.

1. The first and second letters of the text message are short for "see you."

2. The third letter of the message is the symbol for "at"; it is on the key with the number one.

3. The first letter of the next word is the same as the first letter on the key for number 9.

4. The second letter of that word is the first one in the alphabet.

5. The last three letters of the word are the same as the last letters of these words: raves, caves.

6. Here are some clues to help you guess the next word (the next five spaces):
   • It is in its singular form.
   • It is eaten between meals.
   • It is often eaten in small amounts.

7. The next word is four letters long. Use the letters and numbers on the phone's keypad in the drawing to decipher this code:

   | ___ | ___ | ___ | ___ |
   |:---:|:---:|:---:|:---:|
   | 3 | 6 | 6 | 3 |
   | third | third | third | first |

8. The next word is three letters long. Here are some clues to help you figure it out:
   • It is in its singular form.
   • It can be a form of candy.
   • It can be a type of tall stool.

9. You think your friend should have sent you a picture along with her text message. Draw a coffee mug on the LCD (liquid crystal display) screen in the drawing. Make the mug go with the location described in this puzzle.

10. Decipher the code below to reveal the first letter on the next line of your text message:

‾‾‾‾
6
second

11. In the next space on that line, enter the first digit from the cell-phone keypad.

12. In the second-to-the-last space, enter the letter that's the second letter on the number four key.

13. The final letter of the message is the same as the third letter on the number seven key.

14. In the top right-hand corner of both these directions and the page with the drawing of the cell phone, write your first and last name.

15. Take a second to be sure you have filled in the cell-phone picture and message correctly and completely.

16. Rewrite the text message below in English, using correct capitalization and spelling. Note that the exclamation point has been filled in for you.


___ ___ ___   ___ ___ ___

___ ___

___ ___ ___ ___ ___

___ ___ ___ ___ ___

___ ___ ___ ___

___ ___ ___

___ ___ ___ ___ ___ ___ ___!

# 3.

# LOCKER-ROOM LOGIC

Coach Dunken has just realized that something is missing from his storage locker and he has to have it for the track meet after school. Coach sends all the boys to the track to run and warm up while he looks around. Use your best logic to read and understand the directions and you will be a winner in this Puzzle Hunt!

1.  Coach decides Ryan must be playing racquetball after school with whom?

    _____

2.  Next he looks in the locker with the headband hanging on a hook. How many sneakers are in this locker? _____

3.  Draw an X on locker 20 and another X on locker 7 because these kids are out sick.

4.  As Coach Dunken looks in other lockers, he decides that Jamal is probably most concerned with a certain type of hygiene. What kind of hygiene would that be? Explain your answer:

    _____

5.  Find the shoes on which you can see all or most of the sole. Color each of those soles blue.

6.  Find any uncolored sneakers that have shoelaces in them. Color those sneakers yellow.

7.  Even though Coach Dunken has not found the missing stopwatch, he decides to quickly write the two new students' names on their lockers. Fill in the correct names on the sample lockers by following the directions carefully.

**#30** 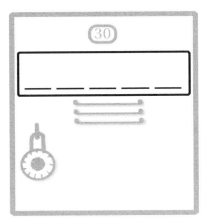  **#38**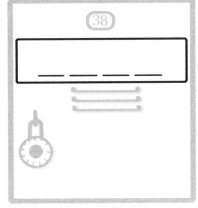

For locker number 30:

8.  The first, third, and fourth letters are the same as the second letter of the alphabet.

9.  The second letter is the same as the second letter of the name on locker number 19.

10. The last letter is the same as the last letter in the names on lockers 17 and 29.

For locker number 38:

11. The first letter is the same as the next-to-the-last letter of locker number 39.

12. The second letter is the same as the second letter on locker number 9.

13. The third letter is the same as the second letter on locker number 28.

14. The final letter is the same as the final letter of the highest numbered locker in the picture.

15. While he's labeling the lockers, Coach Dunken remembers that he lent the stopwatch to a boy who wanted to practice for the track meet over the weekend. The coach has found the answer to his dilemma. The next two clues will help you find that answer too.

16. The first digit of the answer is the same as the number of shoes you should have colored blue.
    ___

17. The second digit is 5 more than the number of vowels in the name on locker number 38. ___

18. The missing item was found in locker number: ____ ____

19. In green, color over the name on the locker where the stopwatch was found.

20. Coach Dunken hurries outside to meet the students. The boys are glad to be through running for a while!

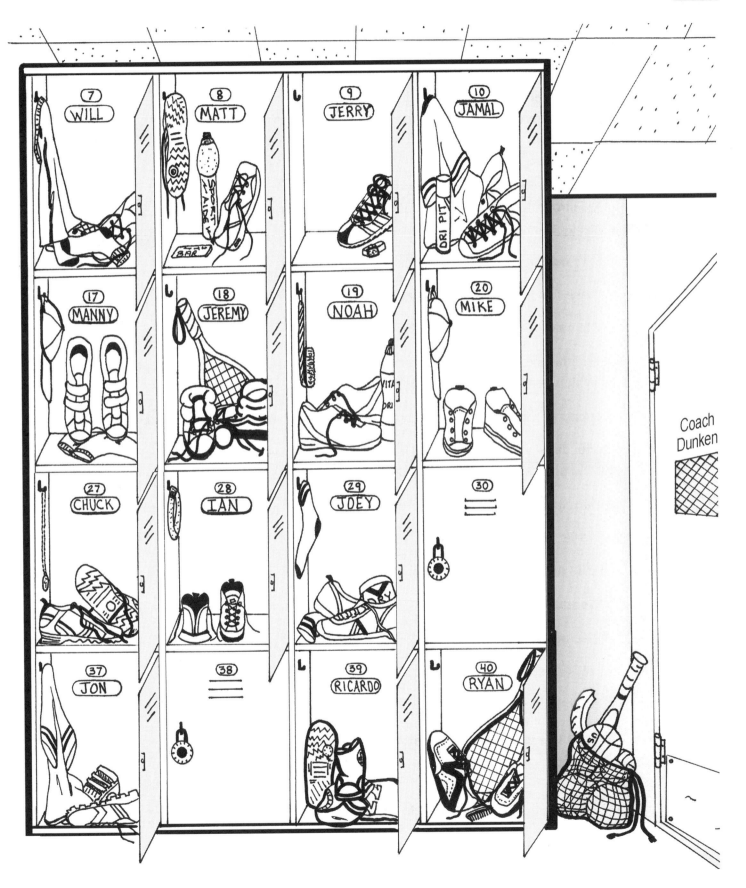

# 5.

# PERPLEXING PYROTECHNICS

Pyrotechnics are fireworks displays. Get everything in this explosive activity right and your Puzzle Hunt will shine.

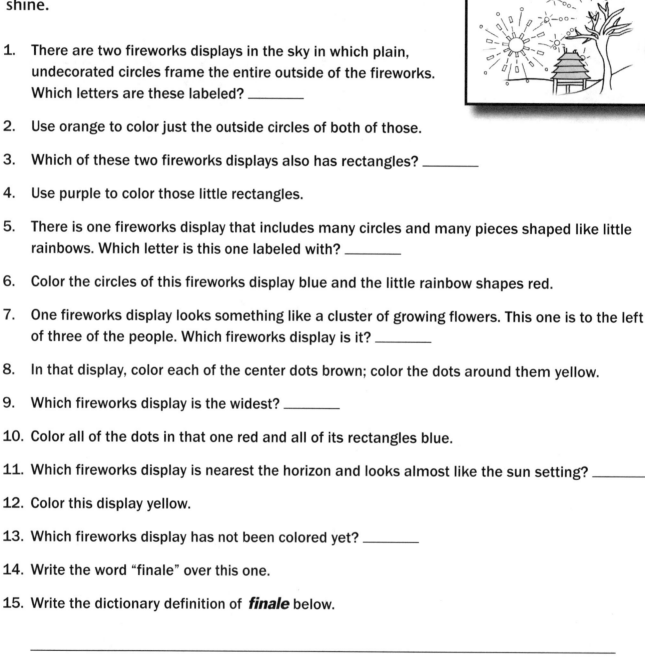

1.  There are two fireworks displays in the sky in which plain, undecorated circles frame the entire outside of the fireworks. Which letters are these labeled? _____

2.  Use orange to color just the outside circles of both of those.

3.  Which of these two fireworks displays also has rectangles? _____

4.  Use purple to color those little rectangles.

5.  There is one fireworks display that includes many circles and many pieces shaped like little rainbows. Which letter is this one labeled with? _____

6.  Color the circles of this fireworks display blue and the little rainbow shapes red.

7.  One fireworks display looks something like a cluster of growing flowers. This one is to the left of three of the people. Which fireworks display is it? _____

8.  In that display, color each of the center dots brown; color the dots around them yellow.

9.  Which fireworks display is the widest? _____

10. Color all of the dots in that one red and all of its rectangles blue.

11. Which fireworks display is nearest the horizon and looks almost like the sun setting? _____

12. Color this display yellow.

13. Which fireworks display has not been colored yet? _____

14. Write the word "finale" over this one.

15. Write the dictionary definition of *finale* below.

_____

16. You've burnt this activity up! Now show it to your teacher.

# 6.

# BORIS THESAURUS

To figure out Boris's diagnosis, you'll need to refer to the drawing of the doctor's office. You'll also need a thesaurus; Boris wants to remove some boring words from this puzzle and replace them with more interesting ones. Solve this Puzzle Hunt and you will know the diagnosis Boris receives from Dr. Iris.

1. Boris Thesaurus fell asleep earlier than usual last night and woke up much later than his usual time for a school day. He feels feverish and dizzy. Use the thesaurus to find TWO synonyms for the word "usual." Each must be AT LEAST six letters long. Write the synonyms below.

_____

2. His mom insists he stay home from school, and Boris is happy about that. Then, however, she calls the doctor. Write three alternative words for "happy." Make sure each one is AT LEAST six letters long.

_____

3. In Dr. Iris's office later that morning, a nurse checks Boris's blood pressure, his height and weight, and his temperature. Then Dr. Iris comes in. Boris has known Dr. Iris most of his life and thinks she's very nice. Using a thesaurus, list two synonyms for "nice," each at least six letters long.

_____

4. While Dr. Iris examines Boris, Boris examines the charts on the wall, starting with the one that shows the skeleton. Color the skeleton orange. Boris is certain nothing is wrong with his bones, and Dr. Iris agrees.

5. Dr. Iris inspects Boris's eyes and says they appear normal. Look for the iris of the bottom eye on the chart; color it purple.

6. Dr. Iris uses her stethoscope to listen to Boris's lungs. She says she cannot hear any fluid, and she rules out bronchitis. Write a synonym for the word "listen." The synonym can be any length.

_____

7. Draw in a set of lungs on the back of Boris's shirt. Then color the lungs on the wall chart green.

8. Dr. Iris tells Boris to say "ah," and she checks his tonsils. Because they don't seem irritated or inflamed, and Boris isn't complaining specifically about his throat, Dr. Iris rules out tonsillitis. Color the tongue on the tonsil poster red.

9. If you have paid close attention to these directions, you will have just one chart left without any markings. That chart shows the part of Boris's body that is causing the problem. Circle that chart.

10. Knowing where the problem is, you can consider several possible diagnoses for Boris and determine which one is correct. Circle the correct diagnosis below, using a dictionary if necessary.

     tonsillitis    bronchitis    otitis media   conjunctivitis

11. Finally, write three synonyms for the VERB form of "circle."

_____

12. As you consider the pros and cons of medical school, show this Puzzle Hunt to your teacher!

**6.**

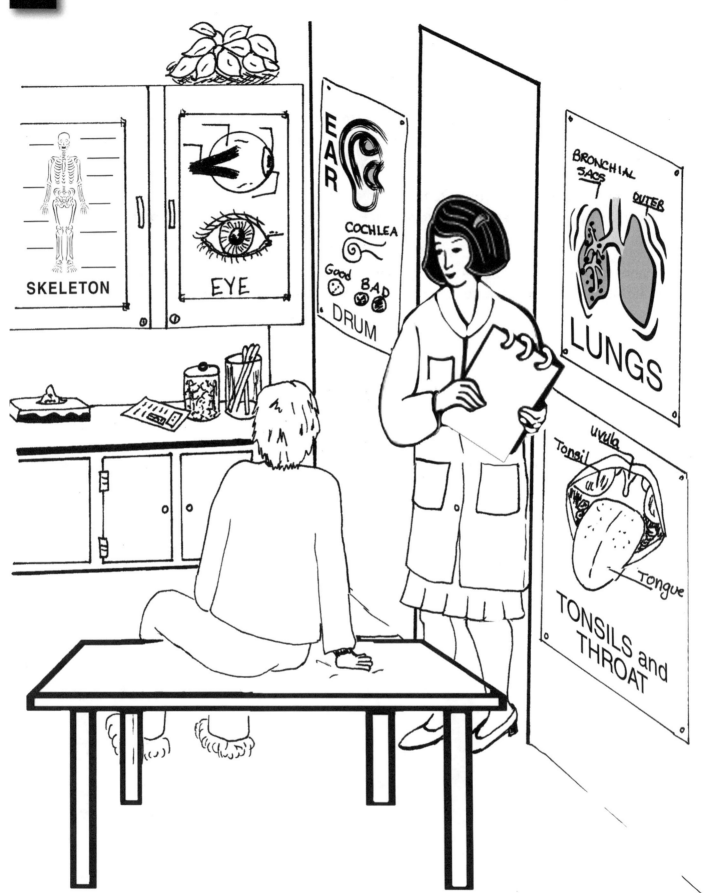

# COUNTY FAIR

Sue and Blu are teenaged fraternal twins who are off to the county fair without their parents for the first time. Below are nine places and things Blu and Sue visit at the fair. Refer to the drawing to correctly match the clues on the right to the nine things or places on the left. Then color the fair's attractions according to the list at the end of these directions. Only when you've matched things correctly *and* finished the coloring will this Puzzle Hunt be complete.

Note: You may need to read several clues to narrow down the one best choice for each.

___ 1. Chair lift

A.  For just five you're guaranteed to walk away with something.

___ 2. Mixer

B.  On this attraction you could measure radiuses and circumferences on four circles and also find six rows of more circles.

___ 3. Ferris wheel

C.  The product of this stand will quench your thirst.

___ 4. Dime toss

D.  Spend money you can afford. It will get you aboard!

___ 5. Air brushing booth

E.  Is it a UFO, or something used to blend cake batter?

___ 6. Cotton candy stand

F.  Look toward the middle of the background to find this. It goes up and down and all around.

___ 7. Lemonade stand

G.  The lemon sign appears to be giving it a sweet kiss.

___ 8. Classic coaster

H.  Give up tickets for a ride at a greater elevation.

___ 9. Ticket booth

I.  Money goes in but a prize may not come out.

Check your answers and then color each attraction according to this key:

| | | |
|---|---|---|
| A. dark blue | B. red | C. yellow |
| D. light blue | E. orange | F. pink |
| G. green | H. brown | I. gray |

# RIDICULOUS RAIN FOREST

You have a computer-generated rain-forest project due tomorrow, but when you open up your work on the computer today, it appears your computer has malfunctioned. Color the drawing according to the directions below.

1.  First, notice the brackets on the right side of your rain-forest drawing. You are pleased to see that the four layers of the rain forest are still divided correctly. With a pen or a pencil, neatly label the four layers of the rain forest on the drawing. The topmost layer is called the **emergent**, the second is the **canopy**, the third is the **understory**, and the bottommost layer is the **floor**.

2.  The feathery plant in the bottom right corner is a fern. It is purple.

3.  Use yellow to color the snake nearest that fern.

4.  Toward the left, with his head mostly in the canopy layer, is an all-yellow toucan.

5.  Red is the color of the treetops in the canopy; the treetops of the emergent layer are blue.

6.  All of the tree trunks in the emergent and canopy layers are yellow.

7.  Some of the tree trunks in the understory have vines or snakes wrapped around them. Those tree trunks are a color that's named for a fruit. The remaining tree trunks are brown.

8.  Color the bananas to look like they have all rotted completely.

9.  In the bottom left of the drawing, find the flying creature about to be eaten. Color it red.

10. Now find the creature that is about to eat the red one. Color that predator purple.

11. At least one thing seems accurate: the palm-tree fronds are green.

12. Green is also the color of something wet that is running through the rain forest.

13. On the ground is a reptile, partially hidden by two trees. You can recognize this animal because it appears to be thirsty. Color this reptile purple.

14. The last problem is that the tarantula near the amphibian is red instead of black.

15. In what layer of the jungle are the tarantula and the amphibian located?

---

16. After you check your work, show this ridiculous-looking rain forest to your teacher!

# 9

# A REALISTIC RAIN FOREST

After you have completed the "Ridiculous Rain Forest" Puzzle Hunt, try this project!

1.  On this page is a list of **_flora_** and **_fauna_** that can be found in the rain-forest drawing.

    Define "flora." _____

    Define "fauna." _____

2.  Do some research on the Internet, or in books with lots of pictures, to discover which flora and fauna have which names.

3.  Once you've completed your research, describe the exact position of each of the following in the rain-forest drawing.

    poison arrow frog _____

    panther _____

    hyacinth macaw _____

    toucan _____

    philodendron _____

    chameleon _____

4.  Challenge: Can you add some plant and animal names to the list above as you do your research? Can you, on your own, draw any of them into the picture?

# THE GARDEN GAME

Hey, careful reader! Mrs. and Mr. Muffet have mixed up their seed packages and need to stick them to the right stakes. Give them a hand and solve this Puzzle Hunt!

1.  Write your real first and last name in the top right-hand corner of this page of directions.

2.  Print your real first name on the left-hand side of the garden drawing.

3.  Cut off the bottom strip of the drawing—the part that has the seed packets. Then carefully cut apart the seed packets.

4.  Quietly ask your teacher to have a glue stick or some tape ready, so you can put each packet in place once you figure out where it belongs. Ask your teacher to write his or her initials on the right-hand side of this step in the directions.

5.  The plants are finally starting to grow, and that gives Mrs. and Mr. Muffet some clues. They think they are such great gardeners that they can remember what the seedlings for each plant look like and label the rows correctly. Write "Mrs. Muffet" or "Mr. Muffet" on this paper above the title.

6.  To organize the seed packets, the Muffets alphabetize them. List the plant names in alphabetical order on the lines below. Alphabetize "hot peppers" as just "peppers" on the list.

    _____

    _____

    _____

    _____

    _____

    _____

    _____

7.  Mr. Muffet is pretty sure the second word on the list above is sprouting in the row where he left his trowel.

8.  Mrs. Muffet believes a cricket has just eaten one of the seedlings in the row of squash.

9.  They both agree that the eggplant must be the hardiest thing they planted because it appears every seedling in that row has sprouted.

10. Use a dictionary and write the definition of **hardy**.

    _____

11. Mr. Muffet goes to his garage to find some garden pesticide, specifically some that will work against ants. In what two rows are the ants most prevalent?

    _____

12. While Mr. Muffet takes care of the ants, Mrs. Muffet tries to figure out which plants are in rows one and two. She decides that the plants that are coming up with veined, fairly broad leaves are basil, and the others must be tomato plants.

13. Mrs. Muffet remembers that she left one of her tools behind when she was working in the row with the eggplant and, to the left of that row, the parsley.

14. The Muffets have just one seed packet left, so it must go on the one row that still doesn't have a label.

15. From whose point of view did we learn about this garden?

    _____

16. When you've read carefully, placed the packets correctly, and completed this Puzzle Hunt, show your work to your teacher.


Thanks for helping out the Mr. and Mrs.!

**10.**

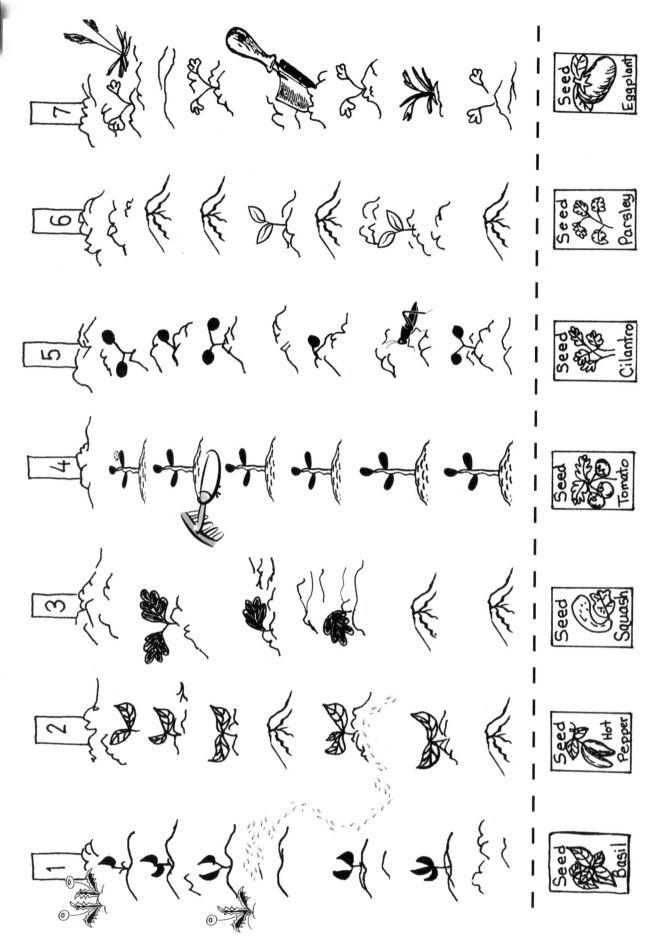

# II

# KICKIN' BACK IN THE COUNTRY

Wayne and his friends have just finished a summer baseball game. They've enjoyed the game and no one's in a hurry. However, after his friends leave, Wayne realizes he's misplaced his lucky baseball glove, and he doesn't want to go home without it. To figure out which of the forgotten baseball gloves is his, read carefully through this Puzzle Hunt. Have your colored pencils/markers ready; adding the correct color as you come to each clue will lead you to the answer.

Hint: Before reading the story, skim through to find the five words that are boldfaced and italicized. If you aren't sure what any one or all of them mean, look them up now. That way you won't have to interrupt your hunt once you get started.

1. After playing baseball, Wayne is **_parched_**, so he goes to the town store to buy a cola. He wonders why the cola case is painted purple.

2. With his thirst quenched, Wayne realizes he is **_ravenous_**. He heads over to the yellow train car to buy a hot dog. Wayne swallows his hot dog in a couple of bites and tosses the wrapper at one of the green garbage cans. He then realizes they both have lids. As Wayne starts to walk away he's struck by a **_pang_** of guilt; he quickly picks up his wrapper, opens a garbage can, and drops in the wrapper.

3. He notices the orange "pond" sign and decides he may need to take a dip to cool off later. He thinks about jumping in the pond in his baseball uniform but decides it would be too heavy once it got wet.

4. Wayne spots a baseball glove on the ground near the black train-car wheel and inspects it to see if it's his. To his own amazement he can't tell for sure. To figure out which one is his lucky glove, he decides to check out the other two he notices lying around.

5. He sees his neighbor's old dog, Spook, and gives the dog's black coat a rub. Wayne can't resist his own childish impulse to jump on the black tire swing, using his old superhero stomach glide. The yellow nylon rope that's holding the old tire seems to give a little lurch and Wayne figures he may have outgrown this old trick. He wanders past the red picnic table and sees his buddy's black bike. He doesn't think anyone will mind if he gives it a little spin around the dark brown, shingled store.

6. The sun is shining off the silver tin roof so brightly that Wayne has to squint for a second until he's past it. As Wayne rounds the store, he sees the three green limestone stepping-stones in front of the store; he speeds up to jump over them with the bike. He clears the stepping-stones with ease but lands right on the baseball bat and skids out of control, sliding to a stop several feet away. He lies still for a moment, collecting his courage to face anyone who may have seen him wipe out and want to comment. Luckily, no one appears to have come along and seen him.

7. Relieved, Wayne **saunters** to the steps of the store and takes a look at the baseball glove on the porch. He thinks this glove looks as familiar as the one by the train car, so he tries it on. Then he walks over to the third glove, near the red picnic table, and slips it on his hand. Now Wayne is sure he knows a way to figure out which glove is his.

8. He's remembered that a week ago he took out a piece of gum during a game and slipped the wrapper into one of the fingers of the glove. Since he caught the winning out for his team at that game, he **superstitiously** decided the wrapper might have brought him good luck, so he left it in there. Wayne checks the gloves for the wilted, sweaty wrapper and then heads home with his lucky glove.

9. If you have read and colored correctly, you can identify the correct glove by this clue: Wayne's glove is to the left of something green and below something red.

10. Describe where Wayne found his glove:

_____

# SPACE RIDDLE

Begin this Puzzle Hunt by coloring in some landmarks in the drawing; that will help you find some of the answers you need.

1. Position the drawing so the number 12 is in the top right corner. Then find the largest planet on the left side of the page; color it yellow.

2. Circle the black hole in purple.

3. Find the double-ringed planet and shade it lightly in orange.

4. Use green to shade in the wings of the satellite.

5. Find the planet you already colored orange. Look for the planet to the left of that one and color it blue.

6. There are eight of these small shapes in the drawing; you may have sung a song about this shape when you were a little kid. Color all of these shapes red.

7. Circle the symbol for "at" in any color you want.

Now let's get to the riddle. The answer is in two words. Follow the clues to fill in the blanks at the end of this puzzle and find out what those two words are.

1. The first and last letter of the first word match the vowel to the bottom right of the number five on the drawing.

2. The second letter of the first word is to the bottom right of the number sign, between two red things.

3. The third letter of the first word is the letter immediately below the symbol for "at."

4. The fourth letter of the first word and the last letter of the second word are both the same as the vowel found below the yellow planet.

5. Find the small consonant below the green-winged satellite. This is the fifth letter of the first word.

6. The sixth letter of the first word is below a star in the top left corner of the picture.

7. The first letter of the second word matches the first letter of the first word.

8. The second letter of the second word is the consonant to the left of the orange planet.

9. The third letter of the second word is the vowel below one of the green wings of the satellite.

10. The fourth letter is being eclipsed, or partially hidden, by the top of the yellow planet.

11. The final letter to find is to the right of the star that has lines extending from it. This is the fifth letter of the second word.

12. Congratulations! If your answer is correct, each of the words will be a synonym for one of the words in the title!

_____

_____

# TREACHEROUS ISLAND

You have just discovered a treasure map. To find the location of the treasure, you must follow the directions very carefully. Remember to follow the steps in the reading process; if you get lost or distracted, go back and reread until you're sure you're on the right path. If you don't know a word, look it up in a dictionary. Be careful; some directions apply to this work sheet and some apply to the map.

1. Write your first and last name in the top right corner of the map.

2. Color all the palm tree fronds brown.

3. Using a dictionary, define the term *legend* as it relates to a map.

   _____

   _____

4. Write your first and last name and today's date at the top of this page.

5. On the map, label the legend in blue capital letters.

6. You search the pirate's ship. Write the coordinates for the ship here: _____

7. Color the three bottommost sails on the ship red. You discover no treasure on the ship, so you continue to search.

8. Count all the coconuts you can find on the island. Write that total here. _____

9. The volcano in the upper right appears to be *extinct*. Explain the term "extinct" as it applies to a volcano. Use a dictionary if necessary.

   _____

10. Color in some black smoke for the volcano anyway.

11. You decide to explore south of the volcano. In orange, write all eight directional abbreviations on the compass in the legend.

12. It appears someone else is looking for the treasure too! Someone has been digging, and that person's shovel is still in the ground. What are the coordinates for the spot where most of the shovel is located? _____

13. From the dig site, you decide to walk across the palm-tree bridge. What creature is waiting for you on the other side? _____ Color it purple.

14. While you crossed the palm-tree bridge, what dangers lurked beneath you?

_____

15. Color these dangers yellow.

16. Go to step number 18 and follow those directions.

17. You notice the grass path around the island and begin to follow it. Color the whole path green.

18. Whatever you just did on the map, do also in the legend. Now continue where you left off.

19. As you continue along the path, you notice the second oar from the SS *Doom* has washed ashore at B – 3. Draw the oar in that space and color it brown.

20. Color the flames orange.

21. In the legend, draw in and label a picture of a coconut that looks as much like the ones on the map as possible.

22. Trace the northern, western, and southern perimeter of the island in blue.

23. Write the letter of the coordinate for the spot where you drew in the oar. _____

24. Count the number of letters in the word you wrote in blue. Subtract one from that number of letters and write that number here. _____

25. If you have been a careful reader and treasure hunter, your responses to the last two directions will reveal where you should mark an "X" in black to show where the treasure lies.

26. Show your teacher your work to make sure your hunt was a success.

## 14.

# SKATE-PARK CONFIGURATIONS

As you read and follow these directions precisely, you will form several shapes. If you can survive the skate park unharmed, you will ascertain, or figure out, which one of those shapes describes you. Keep that dictionary and those colored pencils or markers handy. Good luck!

1. For clarity, draw a line connecting each of the three terms on the left with the picture of that term.

riser

parallelogram

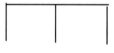

trapezoid

2. Refer to a dictionary, then write the definition for the term **basin** as it most closely relates to the skate park.

_____

3. How many basins are in the skate park picture? _____

4. Draw an orange triangle on the shirt of the skater on Ramp 3.

5. In the bottom right corner of the skate park, write your first and last name.

6. Number the basins according to the ramp numbers already on the picture. Be careful not to write on top of any drawings in the basins!

7. Lightly color the bottom of Basin 1 brown.

8. Lightly color the bottom right basin yellow.

9.  Draw a straight blue line from the raised hand of the skater inside Basin 2 to the raised hand of the skater on Ramp 4.

10. Draw an oval around the only skater who is upside down.

11. Draw a straight red line between the helmet of the skater on the bottom of Basin 4 and the helmet of the boy who is to that skater's right and down a little bit.

12. Draw another straight red line between the helmet of the skater in the bottom of Basin 4 and the hat of the boy on Ramp 4.

13. Draw one more straight red line, this time from the hat of the boy on Ramp 4 to the helmet of the boy who's to his right and up a little bit. What shape have you just created?

_____

14. Someone has spilled a drink near Ramp 2. Color the spill blue.

15. Draw a straight blue line between the inline skater's left hand and the raised hand of the boy on Ramp 4.

16. Draw a red parallelogram around each of the three pieces of trash in the skate park.

17. Draw a blue line from the raised hand of the boy in Basin 2 to the helmet of the boy in Basin 4.

18. Use a blue line to connect the right hand of the girl on Ramp 3 to the left hand of the only other girl in the skate park.

19. Look for the narrow strip of grass in front of the fence; color it green.

20. Draw a straight blue line to connect the helmet of the skater in the bottom of Basin 4 to the right hand of the skater on Ramp 3.

21. Congratulations, skater! If you have read and followed the directions carefully, you have identified yourself as the largest shape on the drawing. You must be a _____.

Take this Puzzle Hunt to your teacher to verify that you have survived the skate park unharmed!

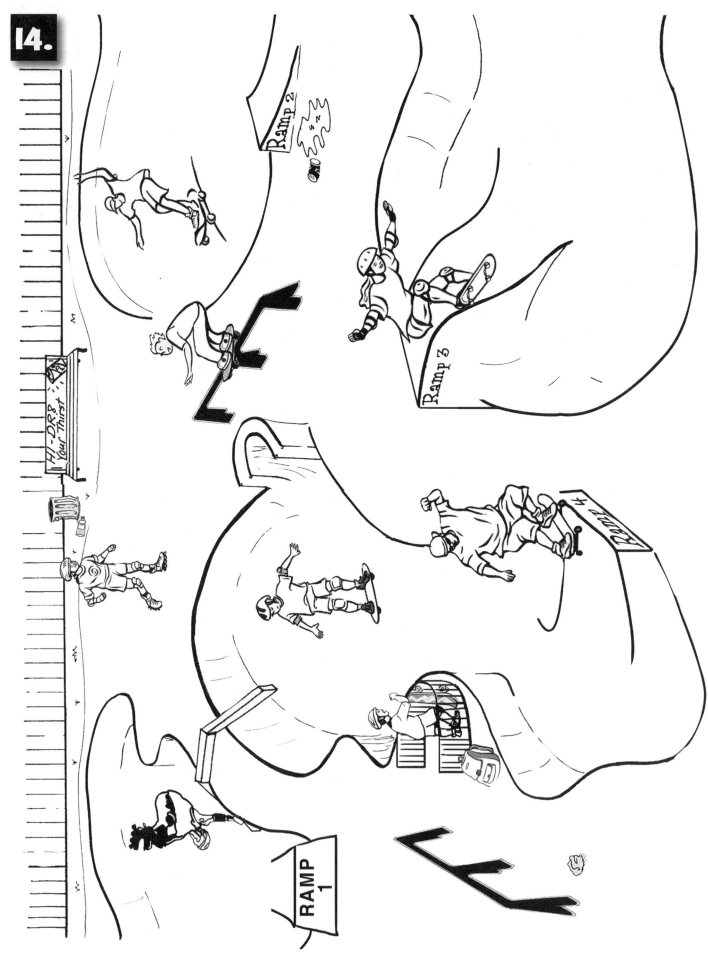

# APPARITIONS IN THE GROCERY STORE

Read carefully through this Puzzle Hunt. You'll find that some parts just give you information; other parts ask you to respond in some way.

1.  Use a dictionary to look up the word **apparition**. Write the definition below.

_____

2.  You just moved into a new neighborhood and have heard from your new neighbors that there is a ghost in the grocery store on the corner. When your mom sends you to pick up some groceries one day, you decide to see if there's any truth behind that ghost story.

3.  As you walk into the grocery store you grab a shopping basket. Circle the shopping basket in the picture.

4.  You begin your shopping at the deli. You need one pound of turkey and one pound of ham, but you notice that the ham does not have a price. When you ask the clerk how much the ham is, he says it's about HALF the price of the roast beef. Write the price of the ham on the sign AND on the line below, rounding to the nearest dollar.

_____

5.  Next you need some produce. You pick up three pounds of bananas and one pound of onions.

6.  You notice that the tomatoes are the same price as the celery, and the potatoes are the same price as the oranges. In the space below, write down the names of the two products for which there are no prices on the sign. Then write what their prices should be. Don't forget the decimal points.

_____$_____/lb.   _____$_____/lb.

7.  In the drawing, add an arrow where each of the two missing produce prices should be—one next to the word "tomatoes" and one next to "potatoes." Both arrows should point toward the produce stand.

8.  You notice something strange out of the corner of your eye.

9. To make the produce look more natural, color the bananas yellow, the sacks of potatoes brown, and the celery green.

10. Next, you grab a gallon of milk. As you do that, you notice something very suspicious out of the corner of your eye. Draw an "X" over one of the gallons of milk.

11. Under the bacon is one product that is not labeled. Write your first name on that package.

12. You go to the frozen-food section to buy some chicken pieces. You see there is no price on the sign, so you go back to the deli section to ask how much the chicken pieces are. The clerk hands you a marker and asks you to write the price on the sign for him; you agree.

13. The chicken pieces happen to be the same price as the Swiss cheese. Fill in the correct price of the chicken pieces on the sign now.

14. As you leave the frozen foods, you notice the candy stand. You pick up your favorite candy bar as a treat for having done the grocery shopping. Write the name of a kind of candy bar on the line below.

_____

15. On a floor tile in front of the chips you notice a small arrow pointing toward the "Employees Only" sign. Draw in that arrow now.

16. Above the gum is an unlabeled box. Color it purple.

17. You proceed to the checkout counter. When you ask the clerk if a ghost is living in the store, he tells you the answer is obvious. Follow the clerk's clues and you will know the answer to this grocery-store dilemma.

18. This is what the clerk tells you: The ghost is not to the right of what you colored brown. Place an X over this incorrect ghost. The ghost is not next to what you colored purple. Place an X over this incorrect ghost. On the line below, describe where the correct ghost is. Then check your Puzzle Hunt answers with your teacher.

_____

# 16.

# KIDS AT THE MALL

Get your colored pencils, crayons, or markers handy! You'll need them to solve this Puzzle Hunt. Your goal is to figure out who is mortified to find his or her mom is at the mall while he or she is hanging out there with friends.

1.  Identify the mom by coloring her cropped pants yellow and the purse on her right shoulder red.

2.  Find the skirt with the ruffles at the bottom of it. Color that skirt green.

3.  Find the boy who's facing away from you. Draw flames on the back of his shirt.

4.  The jeans of that same boy should be black. Color them now.

5.  Look for the girl in the middle of the picture and color her purse red.

6.  Find the boy who is in the middle. Color his jeans blue.

7.  Find the boy in the jersey and make his hair yellow (blond).

8.  Look for the girl nearest the potted plant and make her a redhead.

9.  Turn to the boy with the button-up shirt and give him black hair.

10. Go back to the girl with the green skirt and make her hair brown.

11. See the girl who's holding an envelope? Color her shirt blue.

12. Look for the boy in the cargo shorts. Make his sweater blue.

13. The girl with the red purse is wearing blue pants; color them now.

14. Color the jersey to match your favorite team's colors or your school colors.

15. Still working with the boy in the jersey, make his pants black.

16. The color of the red-haired girl's pants should be light brown. Color them now.

17. You will recognize the kid whose mom showed up early at the mall to shop and pick him/her up: that kid is not wearing any blue or black. Describe the kid whose mom is at the mall.

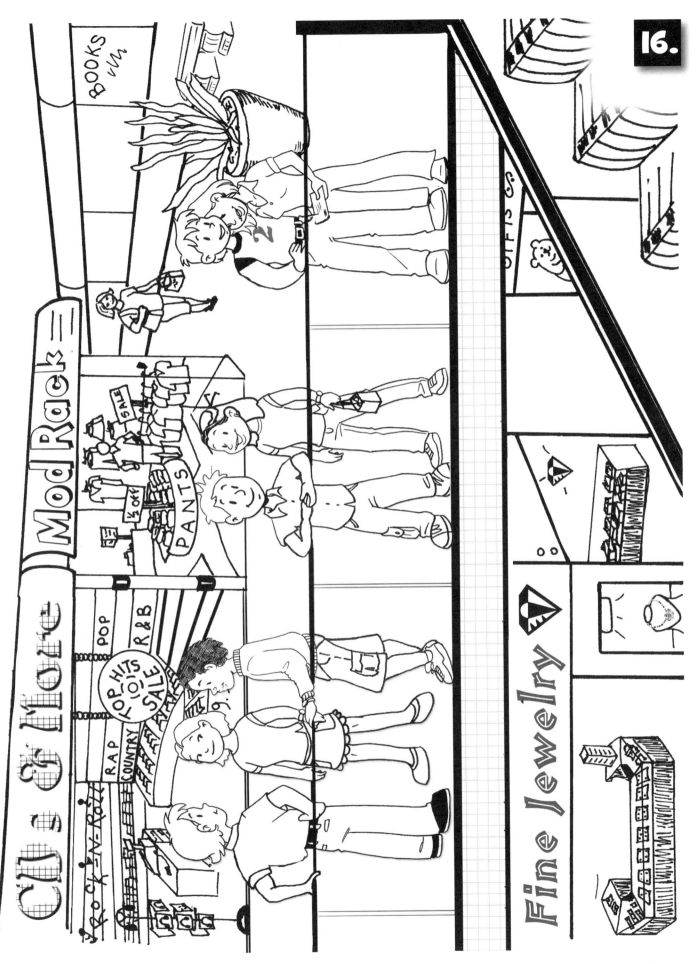

# HOT-AIR HILARITY

As you read this zany story, pay close attention so that you can color all of the hot-air balloons the correct colors and solve this puzzle! Use a dictionary to look up and learn unfamiliar words, and don't hesitate to reread for clarity or read ahead for hints of what is to come.

For Hector Helium, the wholesome hobby of hot-air ballooning was never a humdrum activity. On one hectic holiday morning, Hector **hastened** to heat up his hot-air balloon and take off. He noticed quickly that a balloon on the ground was experiencing difficulty. The fuel jet had **malfunctioned**; the yellow nylon had melted and was lying on the ground. Hector hoped the navigator of the only other balloon still on the ground would stay cool like his cool-blue balloon.

All his anxiety from seeing this incident made Hector realize he was hungry enough to eat the realistically colored fruit on a neighboring balloon. A drink of water from the green-labeled water balloon sounded thirst quenching, but he had to settle for the thermos of coffee he'd brought along.

The orange duck was about to pass the silver UFO. While it wasn't a race, Hector had a competitive side. He asked his copilot (and wife), Hillary, if she was ready to take action and the lead.

Hillary readily agreed. As she navigated the balloon, she happily **reminisced** with Hector about the adventures they'd had while pursuing their mutual hobby. She had insisted they buy their own hot-air balloon after getting married. She and Hector had decided on this one because the balloon reminded her of her yellow-gold engagement ring and they both knew the red of the ribbons was a symbol of love.

Hillary and Hector had been ballooning with the other balloonists for more than a year and had become quite familiar with the balloons in the air that day. Hillary hated the plain green balloon, thinking that at least the other traditionally decorated balloon had bold, vertical black and white stripes. Hector hated the pink teapot because it reminded him of medicine he took when his stomach was upset. He and Hillary agreed that the purple alien balloon looked menacing. They were enthusiastic about flying with the brown camera balloon, though. Hector didn't hesitate to head out in front of that balloon, because the pilot was a much better sport than Hector, even when his lead was being eradicated.

The wind was helpful and the couple were faring well this fine Friday morning. Forgetting the fearful events of earlier in the day, Hector and Hillary flew freely forward.

Vocabulary check: Write the three bold, italicized words from the story on the lines below, and then write a short definition for each. If a word can't be found in its entirety in the dictionary, look for the root or base word's definition.

1. _____

2._____

3. _____

Write your first and last name above the title of these directions.

Take care to see that all the balloons have been colored correctly, and then describe the balloon Hector is in.

_____

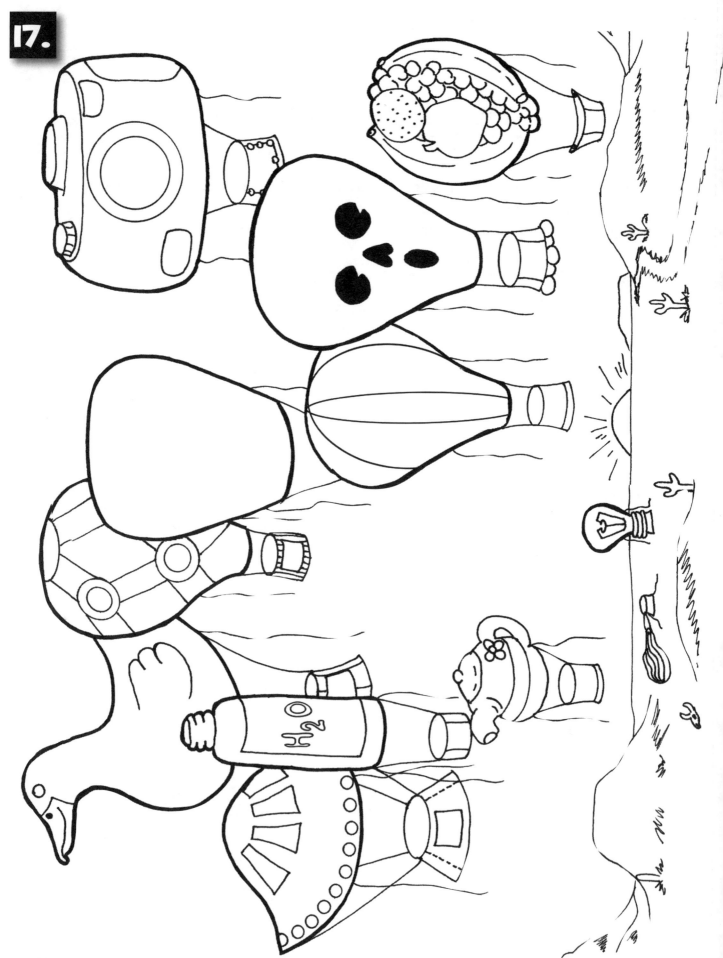

# DIRT-ROAD RAMBLE

Ranger Raul is checking out his beat. Use your reading skills to see that Ranger Raul gets through his shift safely.

1. First, Ranger Raul asks the young fisherman for his fishing permit. Draw an oval around the fisherman.

2. Ranger Raul checks to see that the teeter-totter is in good condition. Draw an oval around the teeter-totter.

3. A camper comes out from a nearby tent. Ranger Raul warns the camper to drown her campfire with water, as the fire danger is high. Draw an X over the camper's fire pit.

4. The camper assures the ranger that she will comply and won't leave her campfire unattended. Then she asks Raul about the Up-Riser tent trailer near her.

5. She tells Ranger Raul that the tent trailer was parked there when she arrived a week ago and has not been touched since then. Ranger Raul calls in the tent trailer's license-plate number. A few minutes later the dispatcher informs him that indeed the trailer's owner did report it missing about three weeks ago. Write the word "dispatcher" on top of the Up-Riser.

6. Ranger Raul next stops at his friend's cabin, located in the top right-hand corner of the picture. The friend asks Raul to help him put in his new mailbox. Draw in a mailbox near the cabin.

7. As he leaves his friend's cabin, Ranger Raul spots a moose in a stand of trees. Put a capital M on the moose's body while Raul enjoys watching him for a few minutes.

8. Ranger Raul stops to help a man whose dirt bike has broken down. Find that man, who is resting under the bridge, and outline his figure in purple.

9. Ranger Raul needs to put up a new sign to direct people to the ranger station. Draw in a sign for the ranger station near the road, below the bridge, toward the top left of your picture.

10. As Ranger Raul finishes his business in this part of the woods, he hops back in his Jeep and heads west to a diner for some lunch. You've completed this Puzzle Hunt when you can list all the different people the ranger spoke to today:

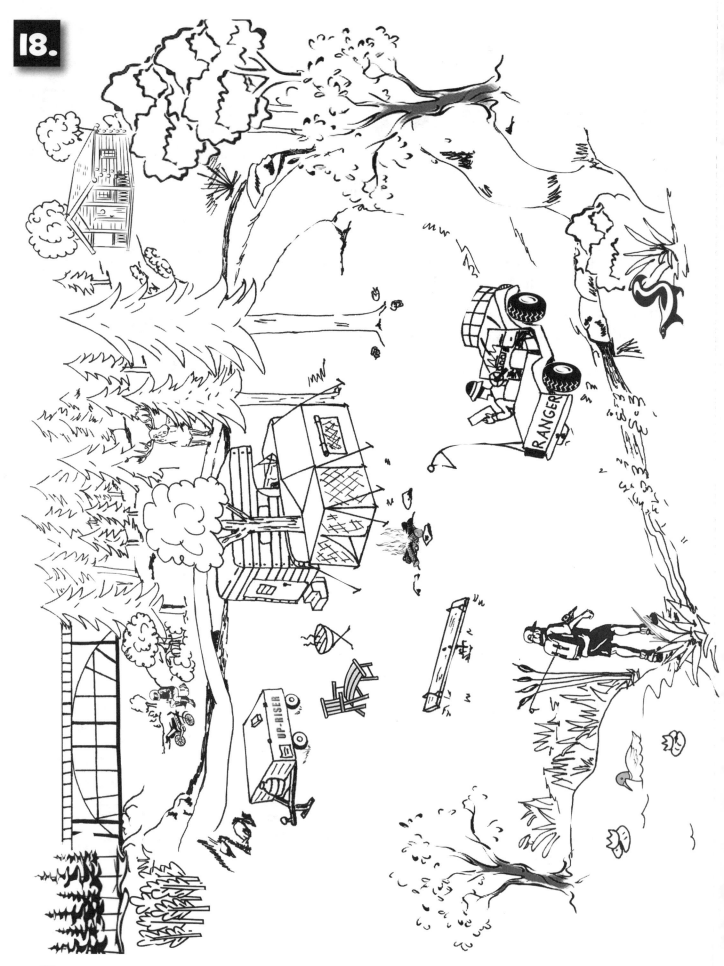

# CUPCAKE CALAMITY

Uh-oh! Your ring slipped into the cake batter and you didn't notice until you had decorated all the cupcakes for your friend's birthday party. Now you'll have to strategically eat the cupcakes until you find the ring. You hope you'll still have a few left for your friend!

Note: You may not need to make a mark on the picture for every numbered clue below; some are for information only.

1. You quickly realize that one of the cupcakes is not appropriate for a birthday party because it is too *macabre* (muh-KAHB). Using a dictionary, define macabre:

_____

2. Color the macabre cupcake lightly in black.

3. Next, while still searching for your ring, you realize how carried away you became with your decorating. You decide to eat several other cupcakes that are not quite birthday appropriate.

4. Find the cupcake that best fits Valentine's Day and color it red.

5. Color the jack-o-lantern cupcake orange.

6. Which holiday is this most appropriate for? _____

7. Two of these cupcakes resemble terrain. Locate the one that you might find in an *arid* climate; color it brown. Identify the terrain that would include a beach; color it blue.

8. Use blue to color the cupcake that looks like a snowman's face.

9. One of these cupcakes would make a great clown; color the nose of that would-be clown red.

10. Which cupcake would most likely be used at a graduating paleontologist's party? Why?

_____

11. Color the above-mentioned cupcake green.

12. What American summer holiday would be best represented by the cupcake that's second from the right on the top row?

_____

13. You realize that your ring has not fallen into any of the cupcakes that are best for other holidays. You realize that because you've eaten all those cupcakes! Your **abdomen** is beginning to ache. Define abdomen.

_____

14. Your brother comes in the kitchen and you explain your dilemma to him. He is delighted to assist you in your cupcake eating and ring finding.

15. He notices that he can spell lots of words using just the letters on the cupcake below the clown cupcake. Write three words you can make from those letters.

_____

16. You are running out of cupcakes to take to your friend. Your brother decides he'll eat the cupcake that would be best for someone who liked **horticulture**. Define horticulture.

_____

17. Use green to color the above-mentioned cupcake.

18. Rewrite the word you defined in number 16, adding a suffix so that it will mean a person who studies horticulture.

_____

19. If you and your brother have eaten all the right cupcakes, you will be able to solve this puzzle. The ring is found in the next cupcake your brother eats. It is a cupcake below the macabre one, adjacent to the would-be clown, and to the left of the only brown cupcake on the page. Color the answer yellow and show your teacher what a great puzzle solver you are.

CUPCAKES

# 20.

# THE SEA QUEEN

The *Sea Queen* is getting close to the harbor but must navigate the waters carefully to avoid obstacles. Have your colors ready! Read and follow these directions carefully to help dock this ship.

1. To help the ship's navigator, find the compass rose and fill in the appropriate abbreviations for all the points of the compass.

2. Write your first and last name above the title on these directions.

3. Write your first name and last initial in the bottom left corner of the drawing.

4. Color the sail any color you want except white.

5. Color the shark fin black.

6. Color the bottom section of the *Sea Queen* green.

7. Color the dolphins gray.

8. Color the sleekest speedboat red.

9. Look for the sea lion and the marker labeled "US12." Color the marker orange.

10. Color the surfboard yellow and the wet suit of the surfer black.

11. Many of these directions deal with coordinates. To help keep those straight, write "Longitude West" at the top of the map. Then spell out "Latitude North" vertically along the right-hand side of the paper.

12. Put a brown dot at latitude 34 degrees north and longitude 23 degrees west. What is this point under?_____

13. Put a green dot at latitude 31 degrees north and longitude 27 degrees west. What is closest to this point?_____

14. Place a green dot at latitude 24 degrees north and longitude 24 degrees west. Who is to the east of this point?_____

15. Put a green dot at latitude 31 degrees north and longitude 20 degrees west.

16. Put a brown dot at latitude 25 degrees north and longitude 35 degrees west. What is this dot on or next to?

   _____

17. Place a brown dot at latitude 29 degrees north and longitude 35 degrees west. What is this dot closest to?

   _____

18. Use a straight line to connect these last two brown dots.

19. Connect the green dots you have put on the paper. What shape do you have?

   _____

20. Congratulations! If your teacher agrees with your answers, you have docked the *Sea Queen* safely.

21. Extra credit: Find the coordinates of the green dots you made and show your teacher where in the world the shape you made would really be located!

**20.**

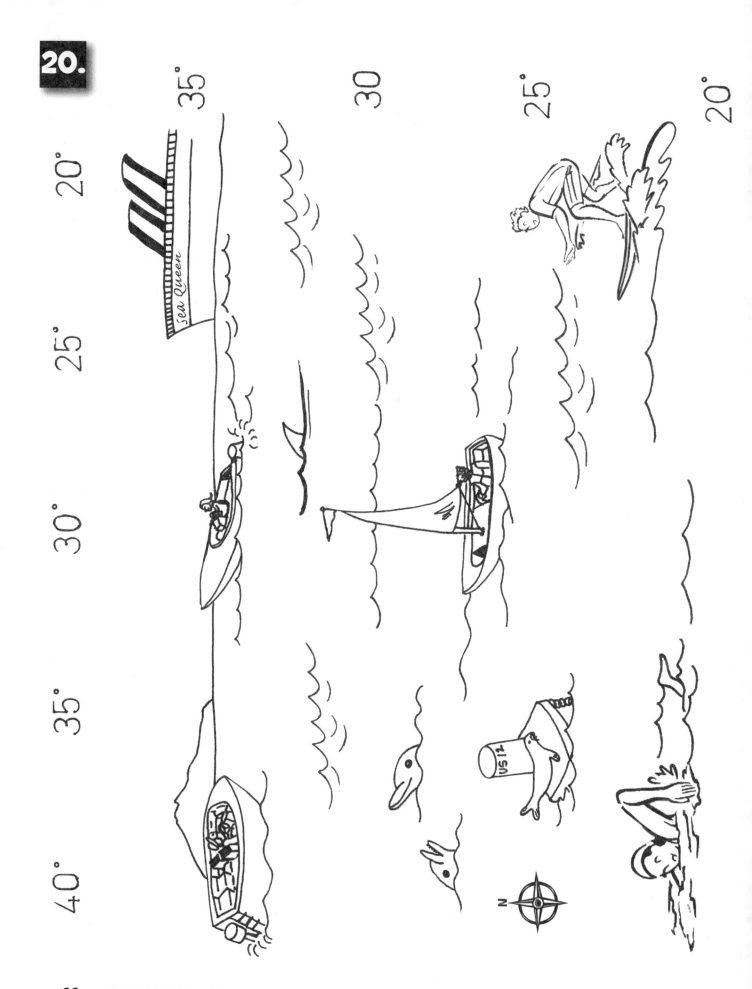

# BAKERY BAFFLEMENT

Get your pencil and markers handy and your thinking cap on! This Puzzle Hunt is all about solving a math word problem. The statements on the left explain the scenario; use the blank space on the right to do your calculating. You will also be adding a touch of color to the drawing. Read carefully!

1. Your dad gave you, your brother Carl, and your sister Jane $20 to share. Your dad said you three are to order breakfast at the bakery nearby and then split the change. As you consider the choices at the bakery, color the drawing: make the donut holes red, the coffee sign on the cash register green, and all four newspapers yellow.

2. Begin the math by adding up the total for the food purchase. Carl orders one milk and one specialty item. Jane orders one dozen donuts so she can eat a variety and take the rest back to her parents. She also orders a bottle of water. You order four donut holes and a cup of coffee. Write the food total here. _____

3. After you have checked your addition, take your total and multiply it by .05 (or 5%) to get the amount you will owe for tax on your purchase. Round the amount to the nearest penny.

_____

4. Now, add the food total and the tax, paying close attention to the decimal points. Write that amount here. _____

5. Figure out the difference between your total above and the $20 your dad gave you.

6. Divide the difference into three equal parts. If you have read well and done the math correctly, you have successfully completed this Puzzle Hunt. On the line, write the amount you, Jane, and Carl each get to keep. _____

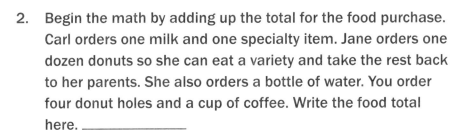

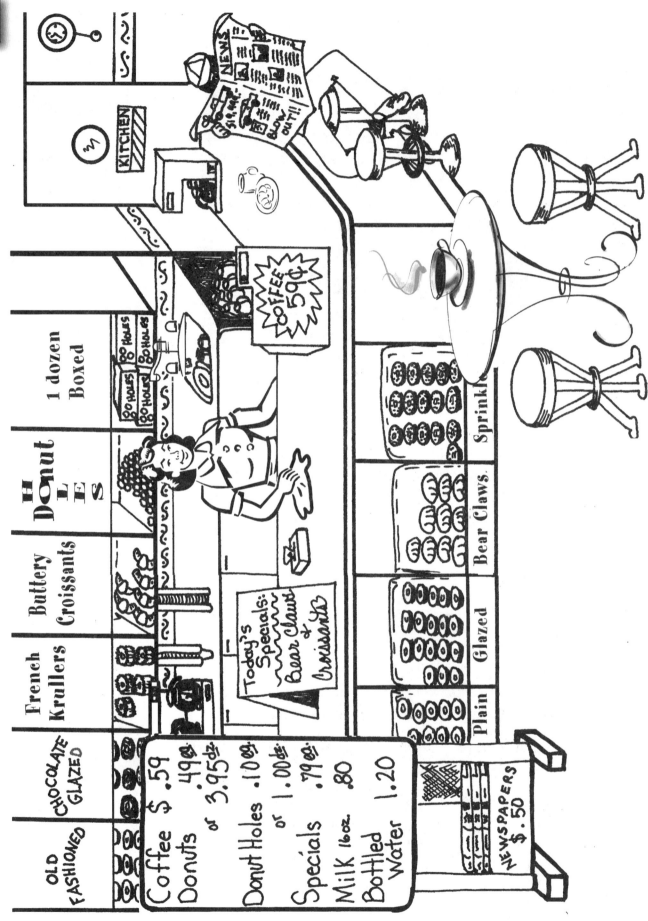

# WRITE YOUR OWN CUPCAKE PUZZLE HUNT

By now you've completed several Puzzle Hunts, so you have a good sense of the reader's perspective on them. This time it's your turn to play author and practice the writing process.

1. BEFORE you begin writing, look at the unfinished cupcake drawing and brainstorm several ideas for your own Puzzle Hunt here.

2. DURING the writing of your rough draft, write down all the steps and directions you need to make your own Puzzle Hunt a reality. Then reread your directions several times. Also, be sure to add artwork to the cupcake picture as needed.

3. AFTER you write your rough draft, go back and edit your work. Never be afraid to adjust and rearrange your writing and ideas until they flow the way you want and your reader can clearly understand them.

When you've finished, ask your teacher how you and your classmates will be able to share your Puzzle Hunts. If you get a chance to enjoy another student's writing and drawing, try to remember: no one is perfect. Give the other student a bit of help with his or her Puzzle Hunt if needed—and don't be upset if your work needs a little help also!

# Answer Keys

## 1. Tools for Success

1. C
2. D
3. E
4. A
5. F
6. B

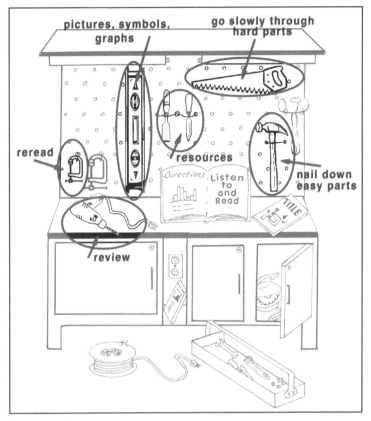

## 2. Dinosaur in Danger

4. "Carnivores" should be circled. Possible definition: "living chiefly on flesh."

5. Possible definition: "feeding on plants only."

8. The diplodocus that is drinking water is in danger from the tyrannosaurus coming up behind it.

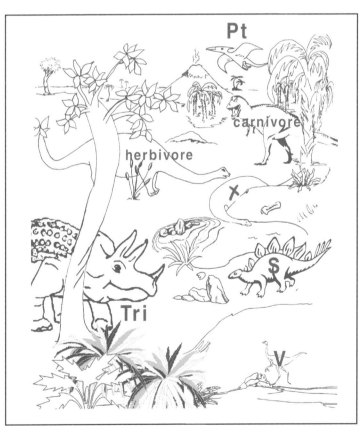

## 3. Text Message

1. CU

2. @

3. W

4. A

5. VES

6. SNACK

7. FOOD

8. BAR

10. N

11. 1

12. H

13. R

14. Student's first and last name should be written in the top right-hand corner of the directions.

16. See you at Waves Snack Food Bar in one hour!

## 4. Locker-Room Logic

1. Jeremy

2. 2

4. Body odor/perspiration, because of the deodorant stick

8–10. Locker 30 reads: Bobby

11–14. Locker 38 reads: Dean

16. 3

17. 7

18. 37

## 5. Perplexing Pyrotechnics

1. A and E
3. E
5. B
7. D
9. C
11. G
13. F
15. Possible definition: a closing scene

## 6. Boris Thesaurus

1. Possible synonyms: habitual, accustomed
2. Possible synonyms: delighted, ecstatic, jubilant
3. Possible synonyms: amiable, agreeable
6. Possible synonym: attend to
10. "Otitis media" should be circled.
11. Possible synonyms: encompass, enclose, envelop

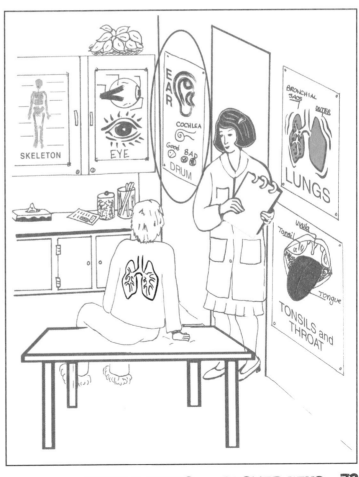

## 7. County Fair

1. H
2. E
3. B
4. I
5. A
6. G
7. C
8. F
9. D

## 8. Ridiculous Rain Forest

(Color key at left)

15. Floor

## 9. A Realistic Rain Forest

1. Possible definition of "flora": plant life peculiar to a region or era

   Possible definition of "fauna": the animals of a region or period

3. **Poison arrow frog**—chasing the butterfly

   **Panther**—in a tree on the right side

   **Hyacinth macaw**—in the treetops/ sky (can be any of the 3 birds closest to the top of the drawing)

   **Toucan**—sitting in the canopy layer (this is the bird with the especially long beak)

   **Philodendron**—above the frog and the tarantula

   **Chameleon**—to the right of the philodendron

## 10. The Garden Game

1. Student's first and last name should be written on the top right of the directions.

4. Your initials should appear next to this step.

5. "Mrs. Muffet" or "Mr. Muffet" should be written at the top of the directions, above the title.

6. Basil, cilantro, eggplant, parsley, pepper, squash, tomato

10. Possible definition: capable of resisting hardship

11. 1 and 2

15. Mr. and Mrs. Muffet's point of view

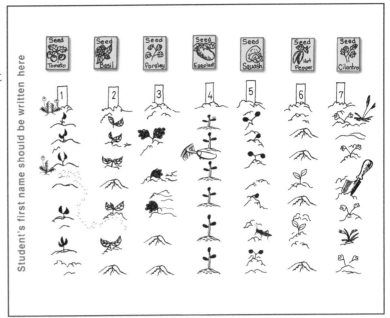

## 11. Kickin' Back in the Country

Puzzle solution: near the red picnic table

## 12. Space Riddle

Puzzle solution: expanse, enigma

## 13. Treacherous Island

1. Student's first and last name should be written in the top right corner of the map.

3. Possible definition: Explanation of map symbols

4. Student's first and last name, plus the date, should be written at the top of the directions page.

6. F – 1

8. 9

9. Possible answer: no longer active

12. G – 4

13. Snake

14. Spikes

23. B

24. 5

## 14. Skate-Park Configurations

2. Possible definition:
   A bowl shape

3. 4

5. Student's first and last name
   should appear in the bottom
   right corner of the drawing.

13. Triangle

21. Star

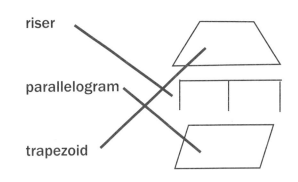

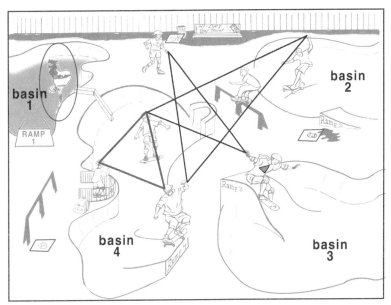

## 15. Apparitions in the Grocery Store

1. Possible definition: Ghost

4. $5.79 divided by 2 = $2.895,
   which rounds off to $3

6. Tomatoes are $.89/lb. and
   potatoes are $.59/lb.

10. A gallon of milk (any gallon)
    should be crossed out.

14. Answers will vary; please be
    sure it is a bar candy!

18. In the dairy case (or in front
    of the bacon and yogurt)

## 16. Kids at the Mall

17. The girl in the green skirt

## 17. Hot-Air Hilarity

1. hastened—went, moved, or acted quickly

2. malfunctioned—failed to operate normally

3. reminisced—recalled the past

Student's first and last name should be written on the directions above the title.

Puzzle solution: The one with the yellow rings and red ribbons

## 18. Dirt-Road Ramble

10. Fisherman, camper, dispatcher, friend, dirt biker (man under bridge)

## 19. Cupcake Calamity

1. Possible definition: gruesome, suggestive of death

6. Halloween

10. The one with the dinosaur, because paleontologists study extinct creatures

12. Fourth of July

13. Possible definition: stomach

15. Answers will vary but could include: was, cake, see, paw, saw

16. Possible definition: the science or art of growing plants

18. Horticulturist

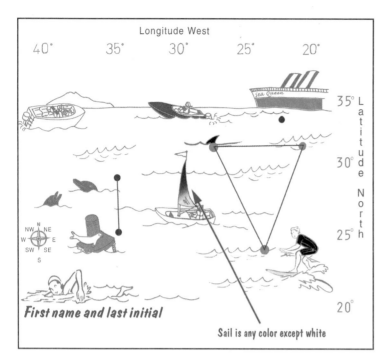

First name and last initial

Sail is any color except white

## 20. The *Sea Queen*

2. Student's first and last name should appear above the title on the directions page.

12. *Sea Queen*

13. Shark fin

14. Surfer

16. Sea lion or the orange marker

17. A dolphin (to the left of the dot)

19. Triangle

Extra Credit: West of northern Africa, in the Atlantic Ocean

## 21. Bakery Bafflement

2. 
$$
\begin{array}{r}
\$\ .80 \\
.79 \\
3.95 \\
+\quad 1.20 \\
.40 \\
\underline{.59} \\
7.73
\end{array}
$$

3. 7.73 x .05 = .3865, which rounds to $.39

4. 7.73 + .39 = $8.12

5. 20.00 – 8.12 = $11.88

6. 11.88/3 = $3.96